20 WAYS
TO DRAW
A STRAWBERRY

AND 23 OTHER ELEGANT EDIBLES

ZOË INGRAM

A Book for Artists, Designers, and Doodlers

Quarry Books
100 Cummings Center, Suite 406L
Beverly, MA 01915

quartoknows.com

This library edition published in 2016 by Walter Foster Publishing,
a division of Quarto Publishing Group USA Inc.
6 Orchard Road, Suite 100
Lake Forest, CA 92630

Distributed in the United States and Canada by
Lerner Publisher Services
241 First Avenue North
Minneapolis, MN 55401 U.S.A.
www.lernerbooks.com

First Library Edition

Library of Congress Cataloging-in-Publication Data

Ingram, Zoë, author.
  20 ways to draw a strawberry and 23 other elegant edibles : a book for artists, designers, and doodlers / Zoë Ingram. -- First Library Edition.
       pages cm
  "First published in the United States of America in 2014 by Quarry Books, a member of Quarto Publishing Group USA Inc."
  ISBN 978-1-942875-03-1
1. Food in art. 2. Notebooks. I. Title. II. Title: Twenty ways to draw a strawberry and 23 other elegant edibles.
  NC825.F66I54 2015
  743'.7--dc23
                                                                    2015031371

9 8 7 6 5 4 3 2 1

MIX
Paper from
responsible sources
FSC
www.fsc.org   FSC® C008080

CONTENTS

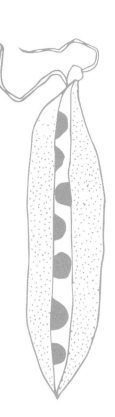

INTRODUCTION

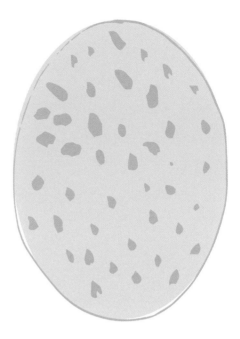

20 Ways to Draw a Strawberry and 23 Other Elegant Edibles is a celebration of all things scrumptious and is designed to help you observe, see, and draw in a fun and interactive way. There are twenty-four different themes throughout the book, each theme exploring a different type of food, ranging from the most natural and healthy of foods to naughty but nice sugary treats. This book will challenge you to look at the varied shapes, marks, and lines and give you food for thought on how you might approach your own drawings.

While I was drawing these pages, I began to imagine all the lovely recipes I could make, not only with food, but also with drawing. Food is something to be shared and enjoyed, and as you begin to make drawings, I hope you will enjoy the process of choosing fun and different materials with which to draw. Add a little dash of ink with a pinch of colored pencil and you could be onto something very tasty!

It may seem a little challenging to find twenty different ways to draw a strawberry, but when you break it down, and examine all the aspects of this small fruit—the tiny seeds that dot it's exterior, the outside shape (sometimes round, sometimes heart-shaped), the curling leaves, the inside when you cut it in half—it all becomes fun and interesting and then, before you know it, you will have drawn twenty strawberries.

Think about scale, too, while you draw as well as line, texture, and shape. This can produce some stunning results. For example, a tiny, fragile, Enoki mushroom next to a huge, sturdy, Portobello mushroom creates a beautiful relationship on the page. Don't miss the subtle details, the not-so-obvious views, and the simple shapes. All of these observations will help you to create fascinating drawings.

HOW TO USE THIS BOOK

There are twenty-four sections in this book, and each section contains twenty drawings of one variety of food all drawn in a different way.

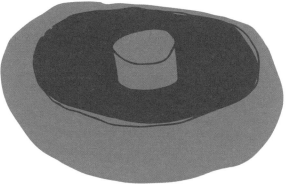

Why not take a trip to your local market and buy some different types of spices in their original state or some exotic fruits to draw from? Do you have a vegetable garden? Do you like to try new foods? Bring your sketchbook along for a lunch date.

You can start by replicating some of the drawing styles found within the pages, or use the examples as a launch point for your own unique creations. Remember that there is no right or wrong way to do it. Don't worry about mistakes! Most importantly, just have fun!

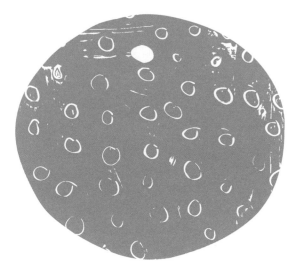

speckled egg: India ink
Portobello mushroom: ink and marker
orange: textured monoprint

DRAW 20
Strawberries

nuts

Mushrooms

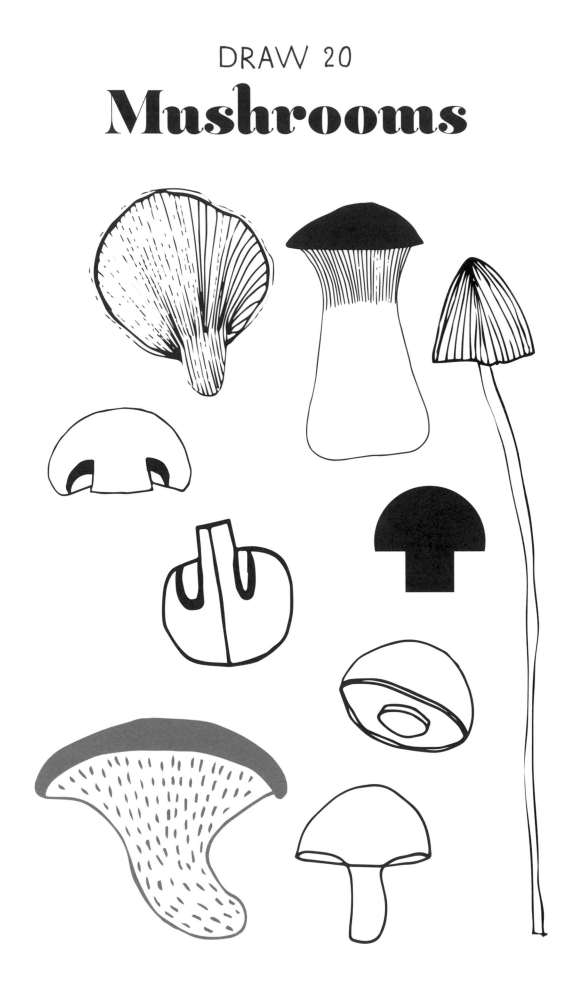

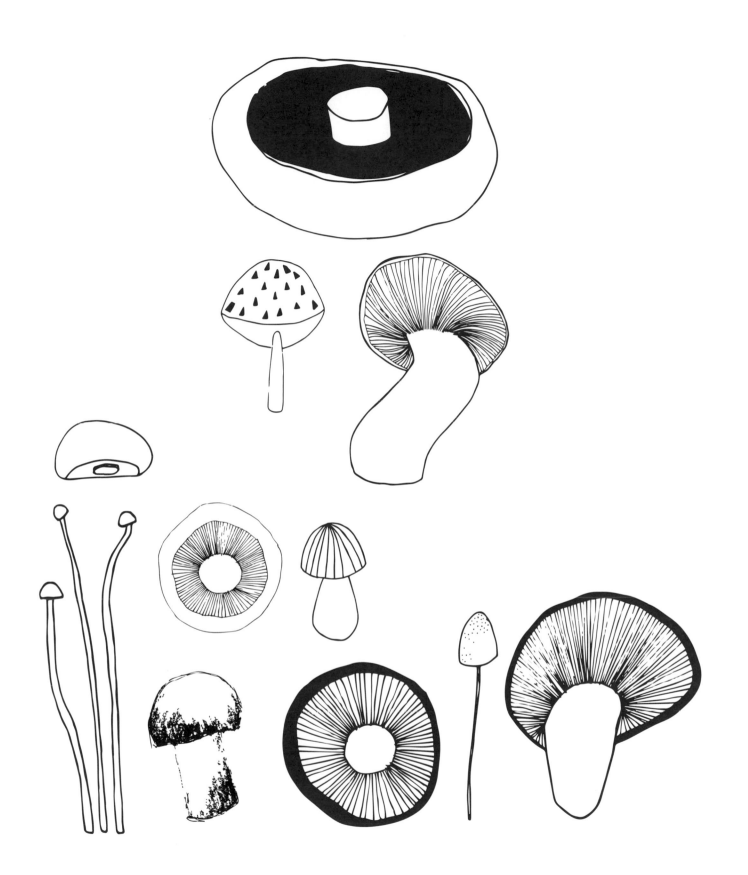

DRAW 20
Tomatoes

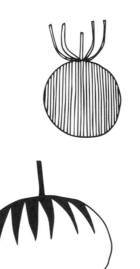

DRAW 20
melons

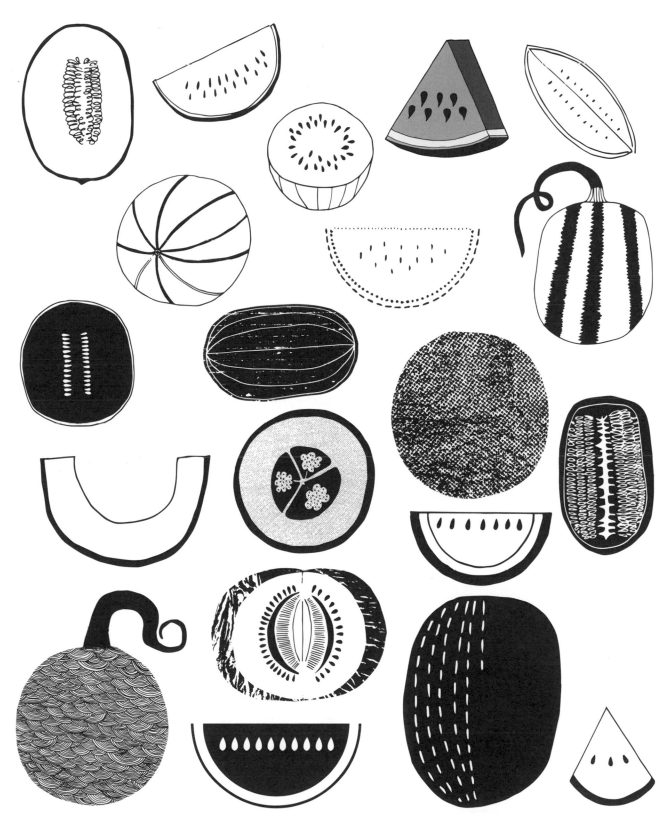

DRAW 20
doughnuts

TROPICAL FRUITS

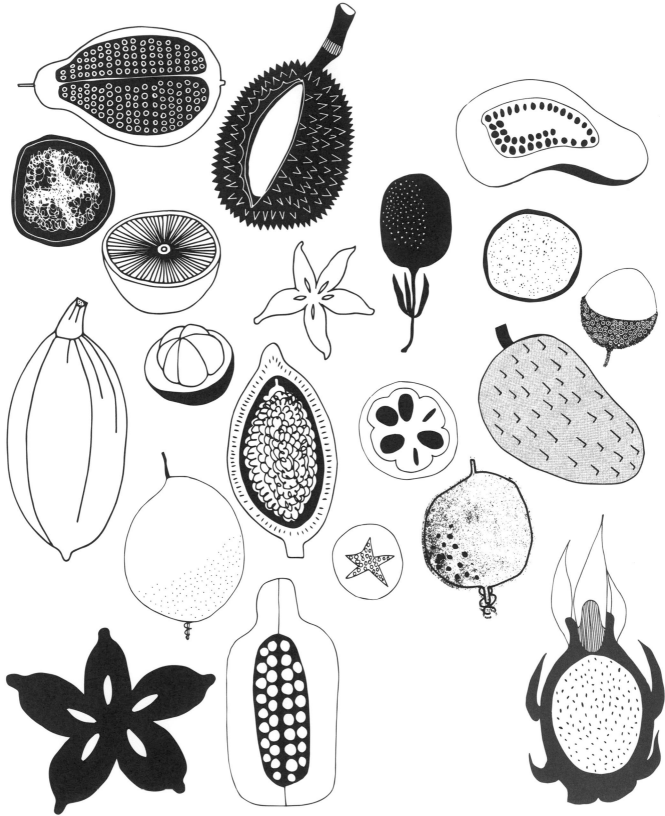

DRAW 20
CARROTS

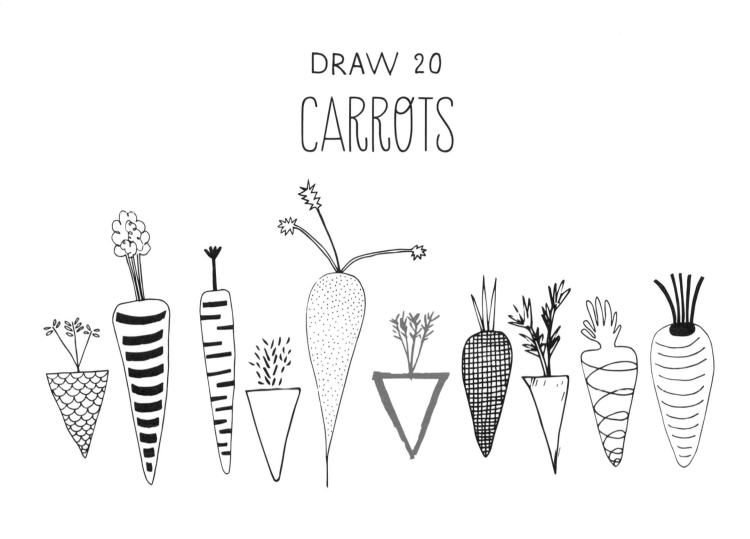

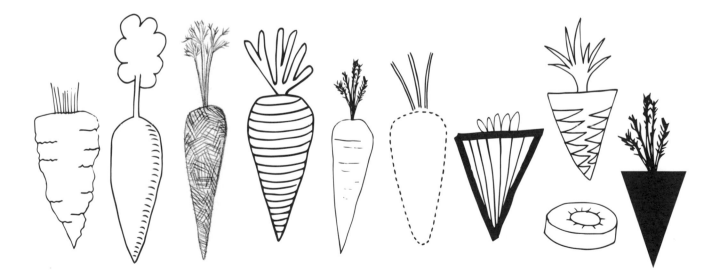

DRAW 20
ICE CREAMS

Cherries

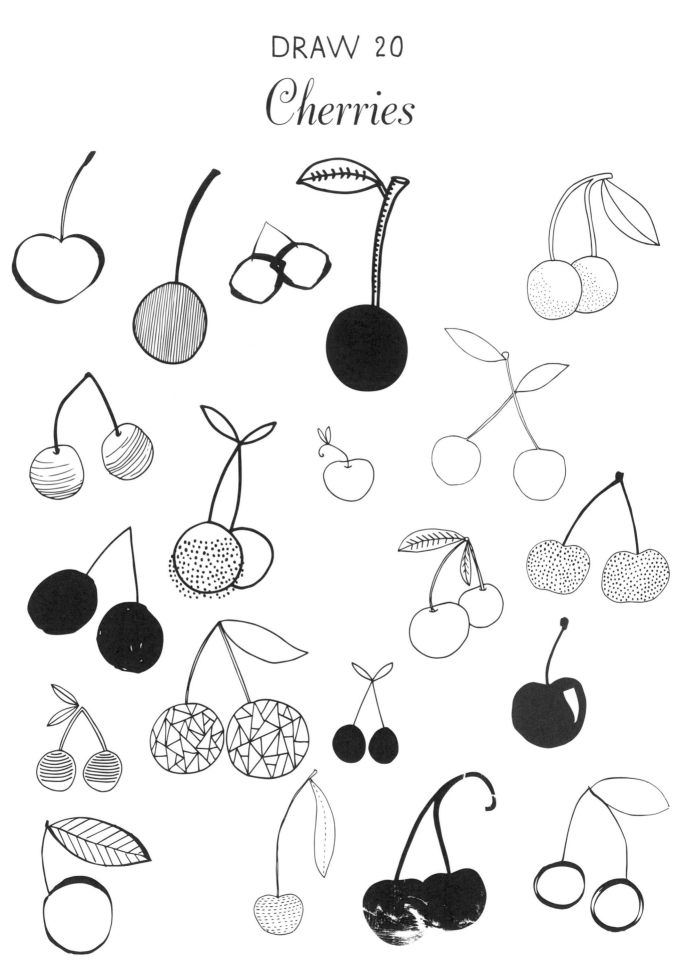

DRAW 20
CITRUS FRUITS

Apples

GARLIC CLOVES

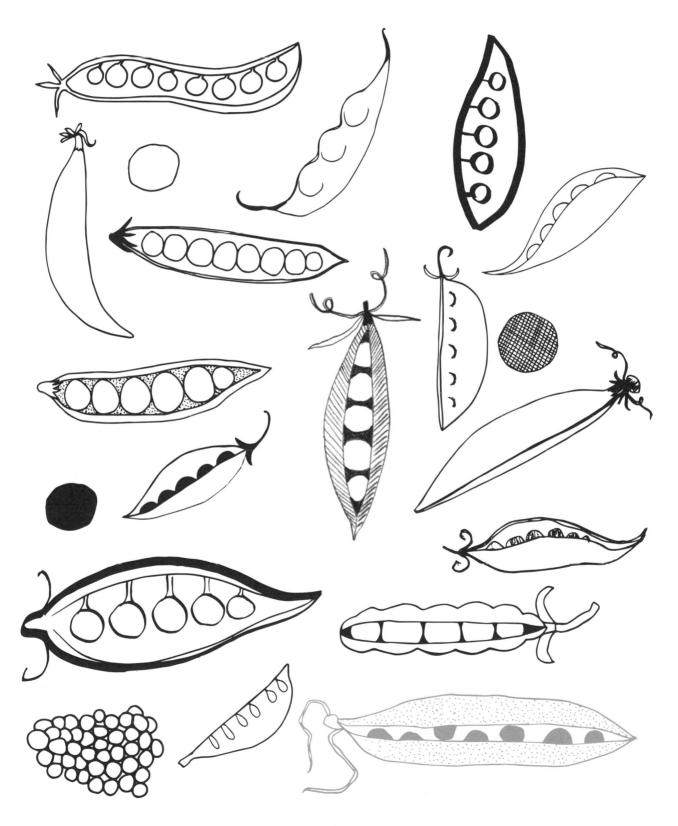

CAKES

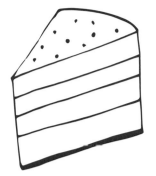

sandwiches

BERRIES

Breads

Sushi

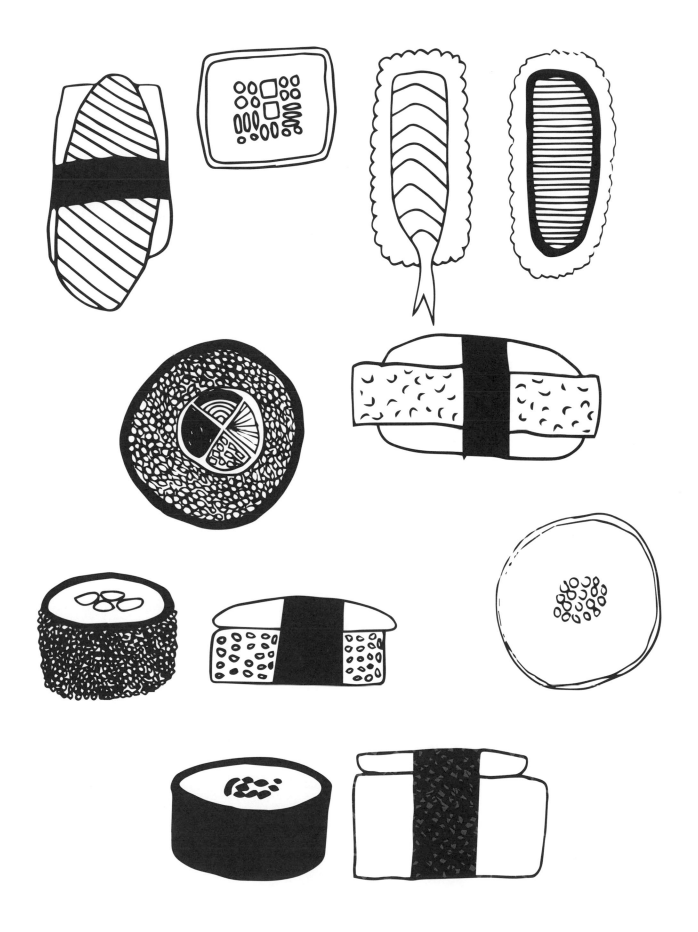

DRAW 20
BiSCUITS

MEATS

Chilies

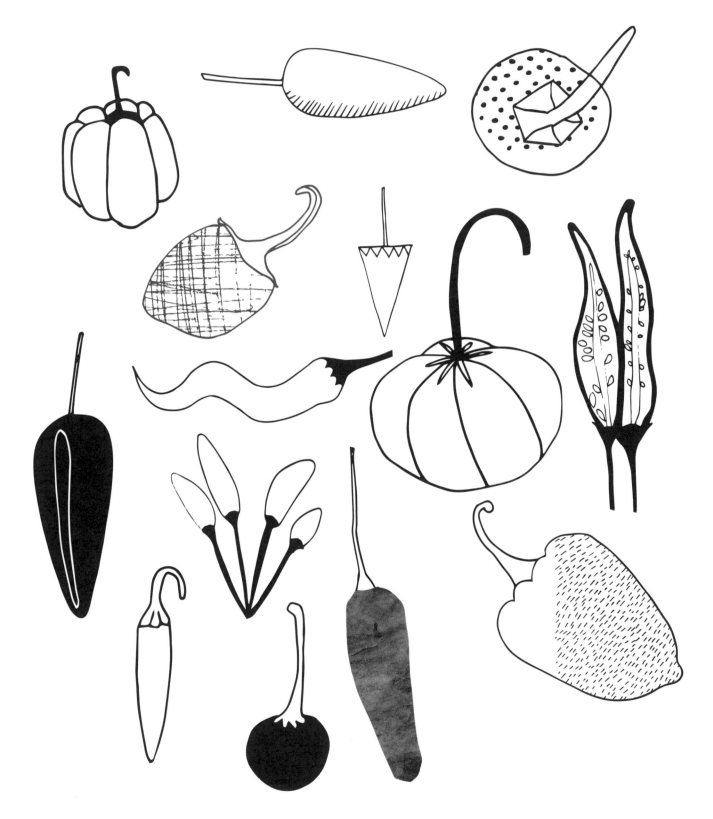

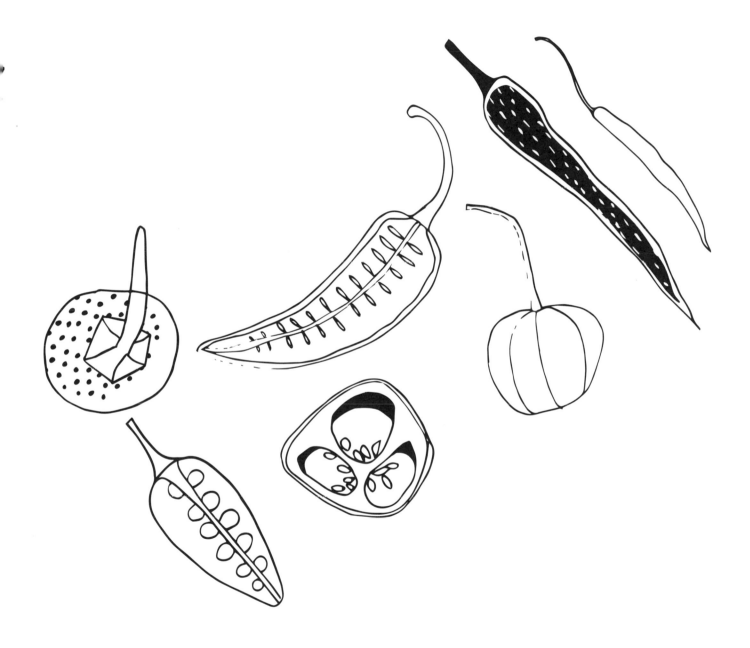

Avocados

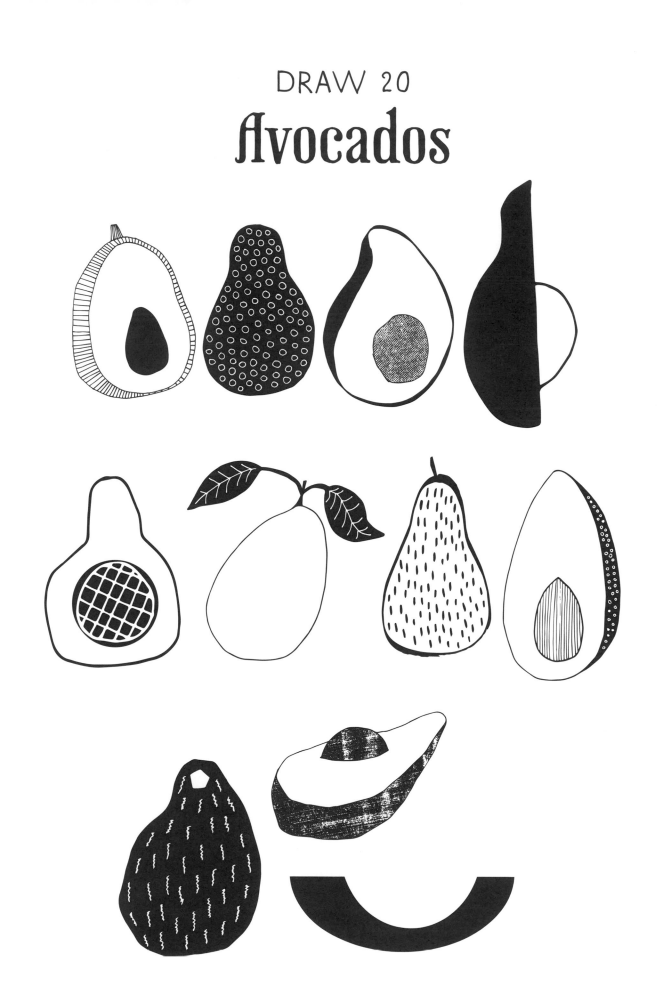

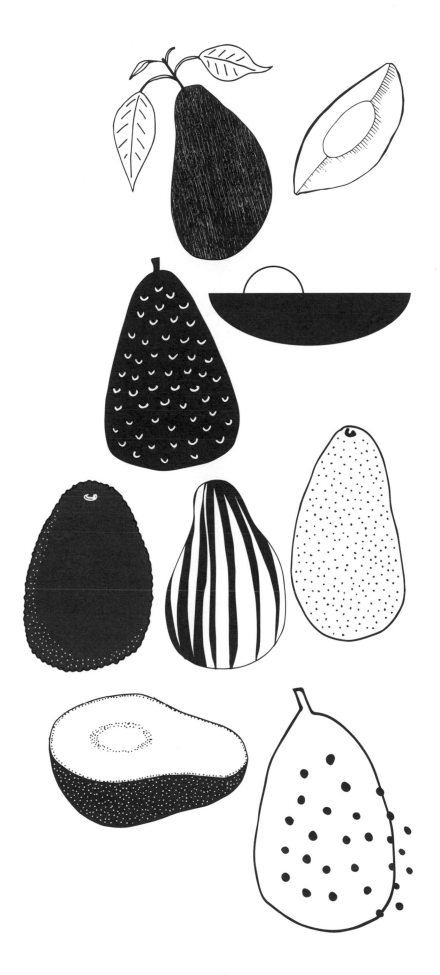

ABOUT THE ARTIST

Zoë Ingram is a designer and illustrator with an honors degree in printed textile design from the Scottish College of Textiles. Originally from Edinburgh, Scotland, Zoë now calls Adelaide, Australia, home. The fantastic weather, food, wine, and surroundings in South Australia provide her with loads of inspiration, as do her two daughters. In 2013, Zoë won an international art competition in conjunction with Lilla Rogers Studio and has since worked with clients such as Robert Kaufman Fabrics, American Greetings, and Midwest CBK and is now represented internationally by Lilla Rogers Studio. She is also one eighth of a talented group of artists and illustrators in Forest Foundry, a global art collective.